T0046700

Who Was
Edgar Allan Poe?

Who Was
Edgar Allan Poe?

by Jim Gigliotti

illustrated by Tim Foley

Penguin Workshop

To Eddie—JG

PENGUIN WORKSHOP
An Imprint of Penguin Random House LLC, New York

If you purchased this book without a cover, you should be aware that this book is stolen property. It was reported as "unsold and destroyed" to the publisher, and neither the author nor the publisher has received any payment for this "stripped book."

Penguin supports copyright. Copyright fuels creativity, encourages diverse voices, promotes free speech, and creates a vibrant culture. Thank you for buying an authorized edition of this book and for complying with copyright laws by not reproducing, scanning, or distributing any part of it in any form without permission. You are supporting writers and allowing Penguin to continue to publish books for every reader.

The publisher does not have any control over and does not assume any responsibility for author or third-party websites or their content.

Text copyright © 2015 by Jim Gigliotti. Illustrations copyright © 2015 by Tim Foley. Cover illustration copyright © 2015 by Penguin Random House LLC. All rights reserved. Published by Penguin Workshop, an imprint of Penguin Random House LLC, New York. PENGUIN and PENGUIN WORKSHOP are trademarks of Penguin Books Ltd. WHO HQ & Design is a registered trademark of Penguin Random House LLC. Printed in the USA.

Visit us online at www.penguinrandomhouse.com.

Library of Congress Control Number: 2015947739

ISBN 9780448483115   10 9 8 7

Contents

Who Was
Edgar Allan Poe?

Edgar Allan Poe walked briskly down a
New York City street one winter day early in
1845. A young boy spotted the famous writer.
Soon another boy noticed him, too. And
then another. One of the boys took a stick
and hit Edgar on his heel. "Caw! Caw!" the
other children shrieked, flapping their arms
like birds.

The moody author swung quickly
around. "Nevermore!" he
cried, and the frightened
children ran away—only
to come back and repeat
the scene a few
seconds later.

The kids weren't being mean. They were having fun, and Edgar was, too. He was enjoying the fame that his poem "The Raven" had brought him.

The *New York Evening Mirror* had printed "The Raven" in January of that year, and it was a big hit for the newspaper. It seemed as if almost everyone had read the poem about a bird who speaks only one mysterious word: "nevermore." The poem was sad, and it was scary.

Edgar Allan Poe is one of the most important writers in American history. He is most remembered for chilling stories that still terrify readers today, more than 165 years after his death. His work has influenced writers, artists, and even movie directors.

Edgar should have enjoyed the glory that "The Raven" brought him. And sometimes, like when he played with the children on the street, he did. With Edgar, though, there always seemed to be a dark side to life. When his poems and stories earned praise from critics, he still brooded over not making as much money as he felt he should.

When he had a good job at a magazine, he lost it by drinking too much. And when it came to "The Raven," Edgar knew one great, big, terrible secret that his readers didn't: His wife was dying. Just like the poet in the poem, he would soon be alone in the world.

Chapter 1
Young Orphan

Edgar Poe was born in Boston, Massachusetts, on January 19, 1809. He was the second child of Eliza and David Poe Jr. Edgar's brother, William, was two years older. He was usually called by his middle name, Henry. Edgar's younger sister, Rosalie, was born only a year later.

Eliza was an actress who had been born in England. Eliza's mother, Edgar's grandmother, had been an actress, too. David was a law student who gave up his studies after he proposed to Eliza. Soon after, he also began a career on the stage.

America was the land of opportunity—but there weren't many opportunities for actors. The United States was only thirty years old when Eliza and David were married in 1806. Most people didn't have extra money or time to spend on entertainment such as going to the theater,

so acting didn't pay very well. And the few people who could afford to see plays didn't want to watch the same show night after night. That made it tough on actors. They had to learn many different roles and travel from town to town.

By all accounts, Eliza was an excellent actress. She was best at comedy, but performed hundreds of different roles in her career. She was lively and pretty, and popular with audiences. The critics called her "enchanting" and "pleasing." David was handsome but dull onstage, and quick-tempered off it. Critics called him "an embarrassment."

Eliza and David traveled with a group of other actors through much of the eastern United States. One night, they might have performed in a comedy in Philadelphia, Pennsylvania. Several nights later, they might be in a drama in Baltimore, Maryland.

They couldn't care for Edgar and Henry on the road, so the boys often were left with David's mother and father in Baltimore.

David began drinking too much and quarreling with Eliza. Eventually, sometime around Rosalie's birth in 1810, David left the acting troupe—and his family. He was never heard from again. Edgar was not yet two years old.

Edgar soon was without his mother, as well. In 1811, Eliza's acting began to suffer. Audiences didn't know why, but it turned out that she had tuberculosis. People with tuberculosis usually have a bad cough, a fever, and night sweats. In the 1800s, there was no cure.

TUBERCULOSIS

TUBERCULOSIS, ALSO KNOWN AS TB, IS AN INFECTION OF THE LUNGS. IT SPREADS THROUGH THE AIR WHEN INFECTED PEOPLE COUGH OR SNEEZE. THROUGHOUT HISTORY, TUBERCULOSIS WAS A DEADLY DISEASE. MOST PEOPLE NEVER RECOVERED FROM IT.

THE FIRST VACCINE AGAINST TUBERCULOSIS WAS DEVELOPED IN THE EARLY PART OF THE TWENTIETH CENTURY. BUT IT DID NOT BECOME WIDELY ACCEPTED AS A FORM OF TREATMENT UNTIL THE LATE 1940S. TODAY, TUBERCULOSIS CAN BE PREVENTED AND TREATED.

As Eliza became sicker, a newspaper in Richmond, Virginia, asked theatergoers who knew the actress to help her. "To the Humane Heart," an advertisement in the *Richmond Inquirer* read on November 29, 1811. "On this night, Mrs. Poe, lingering on the bed of disease and surrounded by her children, asks your assistance, and asks it perhaps for the last time." Eliza was dying, and she needed

help looking after her children.

Two people who responded to the ad were wealthy Richmond residents Frances (Fanny) Allan and Jane Mackenzie. They helped care for Eliza and the children.

Eliza was twenty-four years old when she died on December 8. Her children were at her side. Before she died, Eliza gave Edgar a small portrait of herself. He kept it for the rest of his life—a reminder of the first woman he ever loved.

Chapter 2
Life with the Allans

After his mother's death, Edgar went to live with Fanny Allan and her husband, John, in Richmond.

Rosalie went to live with Jane Mackenzie and her husband, William, and their two children. Henry, the oldest child, moved to Baltimore to be with his grandparents Elizabeth and David Poe Sr.

The family was split up, but that wasn't unusual for orphans at the time. The important thing was finding good homes for the children.

The Allans and the Mackenzies were friends. They didn't live far from each other, so Edgar did get to spend time with his sister. Henry also came to visit once or twice. And the Allans and the Poes wrote letters to keep the boys up-to-date on each other.

It was Fanny's idea to bring two-year-old Edgar into the Allan home. She and John had no children of their own. The family didn't adopt Edgar, but they became his foster parents. Foster parents are people who take on the responsibilities of parenting. Fanny and John baptized their foster son in the Episcopal Church in 1812 and called him Edgar Allan Poe. Edgar called Fanny and John Ma and Pa.

John Allan was a successful merchant. Along with partner Charles Ellis, he owned a business called the House of Ellis & Allan. The company bought and sold tobacco, which was a major product in the region. But it also sold a variety of other goods, including books, frying pans, wine, and even tombstones!

John had come to America from Scotland in the mid-1790s, when he was sixteen years old. Like Edgar, he was an orphan. After crossing the Atlantic, he went to live with his uncle. William Galt was a businessman and one of the richest men in Virginia. John was well taken care of. With his uncle's help, he started his company. But he never believed he had the same opportunities that other wealthy young people in Virginia had had, such as a good education.

John wanted Edgar to have those opportunities. So he sent his foster son to private school when the boy was only five. John bought him nice clothes and taught him to be a Southern gentleman: courteous, with proper manners, and respectful of women. Edgar's first schoolmaster in Richmond, William Ewing, called him "charming" in a letter to John. Mr. Ewing said that Edgar was doing well and that he liked school very much.

In 1815, when Edgar was six, the family moved to England. John's business was growing. And London was the center of the business world. Edgar continued his education at a boarding school outside London. He studied history and literature and learned to speak French.

Eventually, John's business in England failed. Fanny was ill and homesick much of the time, and Edgar missed his friends in Virginia. In 1820, the family moved back to Richmond, and John began to rebuild his business.

Edgar was eleven years old at the time. He was thin and athletic. One childhood friend remembered him as "a swift runner, a wonderful leaper," and a good boxer and swimmer.

Joseph H. Clarke, his schoolmaster for several years in the 1820s, said that Edgar was a favorite with the other kids.

Edgar was very intelligent. He studied Greek, Latin, English, math, and science. But it was his poetry that really set him apart. While the other kids wrote poetry only because they had to, Edgar did it with passion. Mr. Clarke said that Edgar wrote *con amore*, which means "with love" in Italian.

Chapter 3
Trouble Brewing

Edgar's earliest known poem was called "Oh, *Tempora*! Oh, *Mores*!" That's Latin for "Oh, the times! Oh, the customs!" He wrote the poem around 1825, when he was sixteen. It was about a clerk who worked in a store, much like John Allan's. It poked fun at the business world. That couldn't have pleased John. He wanted his foster son to go into business with him.

But measuring cloth, filling orders, and billing customers wasn't Edgar's kind of work. As Schoolmaster Clarke had said, Edgar "was a born poet."

It was becoming apparent that Edgar was a very different person from his foster father. John was gruff, but Edgar was sensitive. John was a self-made man who had little education, but Edgar excelled in school. John cared only about business, while Edgar was putting on plays with friends and writing poetry.

Edgar wrote poems about the young girls he knew in Richmond. He dreamed of having his work published. But John wanted to steer Edgar away from an artistic profession, such as writing, and into business.

Although John gave Edgar a place to live, nice clothes, and a good education, he didn't know how to be a loving father. Perhaps it was because John was an orphan, too. He never had a father, so he didn't always know how to show that he cared. He expected Edgar to be just as independent as he had been.

Fanny provided all the warmth and love for Edgar.

Not surprisingly, Edgar placed women on a pedestal— he thought very highly of them. In his early teenage years, Edgar had a crush on Jane Stanard.

JANE STANARD

She was the mother of his friend Robert Stanard. The first time Edgar met Mrs. Stanard, she was so kind to him that it almost left him speechless. Mrs. Stanard loved Edgar as if he were her own son. Sadly, she died of a brain tumor in 1825. Sixteen-year-old Edgar was heartbroken.

That same year, William Galt died, leaving John a huge sum of money—what would amount to several million dollars today. John, Fanny, and Edgar moved into a mansion in Richmond.

One of their new neighbors was the Royster family. The Roysters had a fifteen-year-old daughter named Elmira, and the sixteen-year-old Edgar fell in love with her. They secretly planned to get married, but Elmira's parents disapproved of Edgar. Although Edgar's foster father was now rich, the Roysters didn't think a teenage poet could make enough money to support a wife.

When Edgar went away to college at the University of Virginia in 1826, he and Elmira wrote to each other. However, Elmira's father got ahold of Edgar's letters, and made his daughter end the romance. Elmira eventually married a wealthy businessman.

Edgar was seventeen when he began college. The University of Virginia had been founded only one year earlier by former US president Thomas Jefferson. John sent Edgar away with only $110 to pay for classes, rent, food, furniture, and personal expenses. John had built up his own business.

He may have wanted Edgar to figure out how to make that money last. In a letter to John, Edgar noted that the two classes he was taking cost $60 alone, and that his expenses were $350 per year.

Although Edgar was two years younger than most of the other first-year students at Virginia, he was popular there. At night he entertained fellow students in his room by reciting poetry from famous authors, or telling stories he made up himself. He would draw in charcoal on the walls of his room.

Edgar hoped to become a famous writer one day, but other students thought he might become a famous artist.

Edgar quickly ran out of money for food or to pay the rent. In his own words, he "was immediately regarded in the light of a beggar." He gambled at card and dice games, but he only lost more money. John was not willing to pay for Edgar's gambling losses. After only one year, Edgar had little choice but to leave college.

Edgar didn't enjoy life back in Richmond,
however. He already had lost his girlfriend,
Elmira, to a businessman. His foster mother,
Fanny, had become ill with tuberculosis. This
greatly upset Edgar. He felt that John should be
kinder to Fanny and should pay more attention
to her while she was sick.

Edgar tried working for John Allan's company but hated it. "Last night, with many cares and toils oppress'd/Weary, I laid me on a couch to rest," Edgar scribbled on the company's financial records. These lines are some of the earliest poetry of Edgar's that still exists. And they show that his mind was often more on his poetry than on his work. He lasted only two months at the business.

Edgar left home and began living with friends. He asked John for money, but John refused. John believed Edgar had to do something useful with his life—and writing was not useful. He accused Edgar of "eating the bread of idleness" because of his devotion to poetry. Edgar vowed in a letter to John "to find some place in this wide world, where I will be treated—not as you have treated me."

Edgar moved to Boston and tried to make a living by writing. His earliest work focused on the beauty of women and on love, especially lost love. He felt the pain of losing his mother and

Mrs. Stanard. And he couldn't seem to get over Elmira's marriage to another man. In 1827, he wrote a poem called "Song."

It was about what Elmira had done. "I saw thee
on thy bridal day/When a burning blush came
o'er thee. . . . That blush, perhaps, was maiden
shame. . . ." That shame came from having
refused the narrator's—Edgar's—love.

"Song" was among ten poems Edgar gathered
in a book called
*Tamerlane and Other
Poems.* Edgar had
to pay a publisher
to print the forty-
page collection.
The author was
listed only as
"A Bostonian."

TAMERLANE

IN 1827, EDGAR COULD ONLY AFFORD TO PRINT FIFTY COPIES OF *TAMERLANE AND OTHER POEMS*. THE TITLE POEM IN THE COLLECTION IS ABOUT A POWERFUL CONQUEROR NAMED TAMERLANE. AS HE LIES DYING, TAMERLANE REGRETS REJECTING LONG AGO THE LOVE OF A PEASANT GIRL.

THE BOOK DID NOT SELL WELL ENOUGH FOR HIM TO MAKE ANY MONEY AFTER PAYING FOR THE PRINTING COSTS.

ONLY TWELVE COPIES OF *TAMERLANE* ARE KNOWN TO HAVE SURVIVED. THOSE TWELVE COPIES HAVE BECOME AMONG THE MOST VALUABLE COLLECTOR'S ITEMS IN AMERICAN LITERATURE. MOST OF THEM ARE IN LIBRARIES AND MUSEUMS. IN 2009, ONE COPY SOLD AT AUCTION FOR $662,500!

Chapter 4
A Name for Himself

Forced to find a way to make ends meet, Edgar enlisted in the US Army. In the army, Edgar spent time at Fort Independence in Boston, Massachusetts; Fort Moultrie in Charleston, South Carolina; and Fort Monroe in Hampton, Virginia. The United States was not at war at the time but still wanted well-trained soldiers. The men in the army were volunteers. They signed up for a five-year term.

Edgar moved around a lot because he quickly rose in the ranks. He was smarter and more educated than most of the other enlisted men. After only nineteen months, he already was a sergeant major. That was the highest rank for an enlisted man. But it still wasn't an officer. If Edgar wanted any more promotions, he would have to go to school and study to become an officer.

Unless John Allan helped him out, Edgar would have to serve out the rest of his five-year term.

Reluctantly John agreed to help Edgar get admitted to the United States Military Academy at West Point, in New York State. It was the most famous school for soldiers in the United States. There, Edgar would train to become an officer in the US Army.

Before Edgar began his studies at West Point, Fanny Allan grew weaker and died of tuberculosis. Although Edgar rushed home to Richmond, he arrived the day after the funeral. It was too late for even a proper good-bye.

Fanny was forty-four years old. "I believed [she] loved me as her own child," Edgar later wrote. For the third time in Edgar's young life—after his mother and Jane Stanard—he lost someone who he had loved and who had loved him in return.

Edgar entered West Point in June 1830. But by his second term, he discovered he wasn't really cut out to be an officer. The academy was too rigid and structured. Edgar became bored with military life.

He wanted out. This time, John Allan refused
to help. So Edgar started missing classes and
ignoring commands. He was brought before
a military court known as a court-martial.

WEST POINT

THE UNITED STATES MILITARY ACADEMY AT WEST POINT IS A COLLEGE THAT TRAINS MEN AND WOMEN TO BECOME OFFICERS IN THE US ARMY. SOMETIMES, THE SCHOOL NAME IS SHORTENED TO "WEST POINT," OR IT IS SIMPLY CALLED "ARMY."

STUDENTS AT WEST POINT TAKE MANY DIFFERENT COURSES, JUST LIKE AT OTHER COLLEGES. BUT THEY ALSO TAKE SPECIAL CLASSES THAT TEACH THEM TO BECOME OFFICERS.

UNLIKE AT OTHER COLLEGES, THERE IS NO
TUITION TO ATTEND WEST POINT. ALL TUITION
IS PAID BY THE US ARMY. IN RETURN, STUDENTS
AGREE THAT AFTER THEY GRADUATE THEY WILL
SPEND FIVE YEARS SERVING IN THE ARMY.

WEST POINT OPENED IN 1802. IT HAS MANY
FAMOUS GRADUATES, INCLUDING US PRESIDENTS
ULYSSES S. GRANT (1822-1885) AND DWIGHT D.
EISENHOWER (1890-1969).

Edgar was found guilty of neglecting duties and disobeying orders. Because of that, he was kicked out of the academy—which was what he wanted all along. Then, in a harsh letter to his foster father, Edgar cut all ties with him.

Edgar vowed to make a name for himself—a name that was not Allan. For the rest of his life, Edgar signed his name "Edgar A. Poe," using the last name he was born with.

In 1831, Edgar moved to Baltimore. There, he was reunited with his father's mother, grandmother Elizabeth Cairnes Poe, and his brother, Henry. They lived in a small house along with Edgar's aunt, Maria Clemm and her daughter, his eight-year-old cousin, Virginia.

Despite the difference in their ages, the twenty-two-year-old Edgar was especially close to Virginia. She called him "Eddie," and he called her "Sissy." They went for walks, enjoyed picnics, and played games together.

Edgar was delighted to be reunited with his family. But he soon discovered that he would have to find a job and support the entire household.

Grandmother Elizabeth was sick and bedridden. Henry had tuberculosis and was too ill to work. Sadly, he died shortly after Edgar moved to Baltimore.

Edgar had tried his hand at business with his foster father. He had tried to make a living in the army. But his passion was for writing. "Literature is the most noble of professions," he once wrote. "In fact, it is about the only one fit for man."

In Edgar's time, only a few famous American authors, such as Henry Wadsworth Longfellow and Washington Irving, were successful enough to earn a living by their writing alone. Edgar was determined to join them and to have a career as a writer.

WASHINGTON IRVING

In 1831, he completed his second book. It was called simply *Poems of Edgar A. Poe*. It was

published by Elam Bliss in New York and paid for by more than a hundred of Edgar's fellow cadets—the students—at West Point. Edgar dedicated the book to those cadets, who had each contributed $1.25 to help him cover the cost of printing the book. They expected a book full of clever and funny poems, and weren't happy with Edgar's serious poems about love and beauty. "This book is a [darn] cheat," wrote the father of one cadet, who had received the poems as a gift from his son.

"To Helen" is one of the works in *Poems of Edgar A. Poe*. "Helen, thy beauty is to me . . ."

the poem begins. Helen of Troy was considered the most beautiful woman in the ancient world. But Edgar said the poem was written for Jane Stanard, who he thought of as his own "most beautiful."

HELEN OF TROY

In 1833, the *Baltimore Saturday Visiter* newspaper held a writing contest for short stories and poetry. Edgar submitted a story called "MS. Found in a Bottle." MS. is short for "manuscript." It was a story written as the journal of a shipwrecked man. He also submitted a poem called "The Coliseum," about the glories of ancient Rome. The newspaper editors judged each work to be the best in its category. However, they didn't think it was fair for one person to win both awards. So Edgar was awarded top prize only in the short-story category. "MS. Found in a Bottle" was his first major short story. He earned fifty dollars for winning and began to make a name for himself.

Chapter 5
Early Writing Career

In 1834, John Allan died after a lengthy illness. He was a rich man. But he didn't leave a single penny to Edgar. John's will did not even mention his foster son, who was still struggling to earn a living.

In 1835, Edgar became an editor for the *Southern Literary Messenger* magazine, back in Richmond.

It was the first of several editing jobs he would hold during his life. An editor at a newspaper or magazine has many different responsibilities. They include thinking of story ideas, assigning stories to writers, and then making sure what is written is written well and has all the facts right. Many editors, like Edgar, are also writers.

While Edgar was in Richmond, Maria Clemm wrote to tell him that his grandmother had died. Maria was planning to send Virginia, who was now twelve years old, to live with another relative. Edgar reacted with surprising alarm, begging Maria to reconsider. He quickly returned to Baltimore and convinced his aunt and his cousin to move with him to Richmond. He wanted Virginia to be his wife, and so they got married. They listed her age as twenty-one on the marriage certificate.

Edgar was devoted to Virginia. They were a loving couple and had a happy marriage. Maria, whom they called "Muddy," continued to live with Edgar and Virginia.

In June of 1835, the *Southern Literary Messenger* printed Edgar's "The Unparalleled Adventure of One Hans Pfaall." The short story is an imaginative tale about a balloon ride to the moon that takes nineteen days. It tells of what space travel and life in outer space might be like. It is one of the earliest examples of science-fiction writing in American literature.

JULES VERNE (1828–1905)

JULES GABRIEL VERNE WAS A FRENCH NOVELIST WHO IS SOMETIMES REFERRED TO AS THE FATHER OF SCIENCE FICTION. HE IS BEST KNOWN FOR HIS NOVEL *TWENTY THOUSAND LEAGUES UNDER THE SEA*, WHICH RECOUNTS THE ADVENTURES OF CAPTAIN NEMO ABOARD HIS SUBMARINE *THE NAUTILUS*. BUT HIS EARLIER WORK, INCLUDING *FROM THE EARTH TO THE MOON* AND *FIVE WEEKS IN A BALLOON*, WERE GREATLY INFLUENCED BY EDGAR ALLAN POE AND "THE UNPARALLELED ADVENTURE OF ONE HANS PFAALL."

In his seventeen months at the *Southern Literary Messenger*, Edgar became one of America's leading literary critics. He wrote honest, but sometimes brutal, reviews of other writers' stories and books. He was occasionally so harsh that he was nicknamed the "Tomahawk Man." A tomahawk is a type of hatchet, and a negative review is sometimes called "a hatchet job." Fellow writers may not have liked some of Poe's reviews, but readers apparently did: The *Southern Literary Messenger* reportedly increased its number of subscriptions from 700 to 5,500 in Edgar's time there.

But reviewing other writers' stories and working as an editor left Edgar little time for writing of his own. So he left the *Southern Literary*

Messenger in 1837 to move with Virginia and
Maria Clemm to Philadelphia and concentrate on
his writing.

In 1838, Harper & Brothers in New York published *The Narrative of Arthur Gordon Pym of Nantucket*. It was Edgar's first, and only, complete novel. He wrote the book—about a stowaway on a whaling ship who has a series of outrageous adventures—because he was having trouble selling his short stories.

And when the novel received mostly poor reviews, Edgar agreed. He called it a "silly book."

The Narrative of Arthur Gordon Pym of Nantucket told tales of suffering and death, and even cannibalism. Edgar had already witnessed plenty of suffering and death in his lifetime. He began to write more and more about very sad, and sometimes scary, subjects.

In 1839, *Burton's Gentlemen's Magazine* published "The Fall of the House of Usher." The terrifying gothic story of the twins Roderick and Madeline Usher and their creepy old mansion became hugely popular. The story made Edgar famous.

GOTHIC FICTION

GOTHIC FICTION IS A TYPE OF STORY THAT ORIGINATED IN ENGLAND IN THE LATE EIGHTEENTH CENTURY. ONE OF THE MOST FAMOUS EARLY GOTHIC NOVELS IS MARY SHELLEY'S *FRANKENSTEIN*, PUBLISHED IN 1818.

THE WORD *GOTHIC* REFERS TO A STYLE OF GLOOMY BUILDINGS (SUCH AS MANY MEDIEVAL CASTLES AND COUNTRY ESTATES) WHERE THESE STORIES TAKE PLACE. A GOTHIC STORY COMBINES ROMANCE, HORROR, AND THE SUPERNATURAL, AND OFTEN LEAVES ITS READER WITH A SENSE OF TERROR OR DREAD.

"The Fall of the House of Usher" was reprinted in a book of Edgar's stories, called *Tales of the Grotesque and Arabesque,* in 1840. But the publisher didn't have the money to pay him cash for his work. He had to settle for twenty free copies of the book as payment. Although he was now famous throughout the United States, Edgar was still struggling to earn his living as a writer.

Chapter 6
Triumph and Tragedy

Edgar returned to work as an editor. While living in Philadelphia, he worked at *Burton's Gentlemen's Magazine* and *Graham's Magazine*. He kept his reputation as a highly regarded critic, while also writing some of his own poems and short stories.

In 1841, Edgar wrote a short story called "The Murders in the Rue Morgue," for *Graham's Magazine*. In it, an amateur detective named C. Auguste Dupin uses both logic and imagination to solve a series of murders that the police cannot.

"The Murders in the Rue Morgue" was a huge hit with *Graham's Magazine* readers. There had never been a mystery about the reasoning powers of the hero. Mystery stories had always been about action. With "The Murders in the Rue Morgue," Edgar had created the very first detective mystery!

His character Dupin was the model on which future famous literary detectives such as Sir Arthur

Conan Doyle's Sherlock Holmes and Agatha Christie's Hercule Poirot were based. Dupin returned in two more of Edgar's short stories: "The Mystery of Marie Rogêt" (1842) and "The Purloined Letter" (1844).

Edgar's feeling of triumph with "The Murders in the Rue Morgue" was short-lived. In 1842, Virginia was singing for Edgar and some friends when she began coughing up blood.

WHO'S NUMBER ONE?

C. AUGUSTE DUPIN MAY HAVE BEEN THE *FIRST* LITERARY DETECTIVE, BUT HE'S NOT THE MOST FAMOUS. THAT TITLE UNDOUBTEDLY BELONGS TO SHERLOCK HOLMES.

ENGLISH AUTHOR SIR ARTHUR CONAN DOYLE CREATED HOLMES IN 1887. THAT WAS NEARLY FIFTY YEARS AFTER EDGAR ALLAN POE WROTE "THE MURDERS IN THE RUE MORGUE." WITH THE HELP OF HIS FRIEND AND ASSISTANT DR. WATSON, SHERLOCK HOLMES USES LOGIC TO SOLVE CRIMES IN FOUR NOVELS AND FIFTY-SIX SHORT STORIES.

SHERLOCK HOLMES

Edgar's worst fears soon were confirmed. Virginia had tuberculosis—the same disease that killed his mother, his brother, and his foster mother. Virginia rallied after her first bout of tuberculosis, but she was often sick the rest of her life.

Edgar left *Graham's Magazine* and moved with Virginia and Maria Clemm to New York. In the Bronx, which at that time was in the countryside just north of New York City, they rented a small, peaceful cottage where Virginia could rest and Edgar could concentrate. He wrote more and more,

trying to make enough money to pay the bills.
Edgar never seemed to stay in one place for very
long. He switched jobs frequently. Sometimes,

he didn't get along with his bosses. Other times, he was fired for drinking. And on other occasions, he was completely exhausted from working long hours.

HENRY WADSWORTH LONGFELLOW
(1807–1887)

HENRY WADSWORTH LONGFELLOW WAS BORN IN PORTLAND, MAINE, AND BEGAN HIS CAREER AS A TEACHER. HE WENT ON TO BECOME THE MOST FAMOUS AMERICAN POET OF HIS TIME. HE IS KNOWN FOR LYRIC POETRY THAT FEATURES STORIES FROM MYTHS AND LEGENDS. LONGFELLOW'S MOST FAMOUS POEMS ARE "PAUL REVERE'S RIDE" AND *THE SONG OF HIAWATHA* AND *EVANGELINE*, WHICH ARE CALLED "EPIC" POEMS BECAUSE THEY ARE QUITE LONG.

HENRY WADSWORTH LONGFELLOW

Edgar sometimes picked fights with other writers and editors. He once accused the famous poet Henry Wadsworth Longfellow of plagiarism. Today, plagiarism means copying other people's work. It's a serious accusation. However, the word had a slightly different meaning in Edgar's time. It meant lacking original ideas, rather than copying someone else's writing word for word.

Some writers rushed to Longfellow's defense. Others believed Edgar was right. Longfellow refused to answer Edgar's accusations. And some people thought the whole scandal was a publicity stunt to sell magazines.

While he was editing, Edgar was also still writing his own poems and short stories, and taking care of his wife.

Clearly, the difficulty Edgar was facing in his life made his poems and stories even more gloomy. He worried all the time about Virginia's health. Several times she was near death. Then

she seemed to get better, and his hopes were raised.
But sooner or later she would fall sick again and
Edgar would then become even more depressed.

Even so, the decade of the 1840s brought with it some of Edgar's finest and most famous work. Some of his stories included grim images of death or murder. Yet that's not always what made them so terrifying. Instead, it was the chilling sense of despair Edgar created. It played up the reader's fear of the unknown.

In 1842, Edgar wrote "The Masque of the Red Death." The short story is about a terrible plague that claims its victims during a masked ball.

In June 1843, Edgar won a short-story contest in the *Philadelphia Dollar Newspaper*. "The Gold Bug" was a story about hidden pirate treasure that contained a secret message hidden in code.

"The Gold Bug" was one of the most widely read of Edgar's stories or poems during his lifetime. It helped sell out all copies of the *Dollar*.

Because it was so popular, other writers also began to create stories that featured secret writing and code-breaking. Edgar's first prize was one hundred dollars, probably the largest amount he had ever received for any of his works.

More of Edgar's most famous short stories followed: In "The Tell-Tale Heart," the person telling the story—the narrator—has gone insane after killing a man. "The Pit and the Pendulum" tells the story of a condemned man suffering in a torture chamber. In "The Cask of Amontillado," the storyteller takes revenge on a rival by burying him alive.

Then Edgar had his greatest literary triumph. In 1845, the *New York Evening Mirror* published his poem "The Raven." Edgar already was well known, but "The Raven" made him a full-fledged celebrity. He was invited to the parties of important people in New York City, where he was considered funny, smart, and entertaining. He was asked to give poetry readings and lectures for large audiences.

Unfortunately, "The Raven" also hinted at what was to come for Edgar. The storyteller in "The Raven" was a poet who longed to hold his lost love

THE RAVEN

ONCE UPON A MIDNIGHT DREARY,
WHILE I PONDERED, WEAK AND WEARY,
    OVER MANY A QUAINT AND CURIOUS
VOLUME OF FORGOTTEN LORE—
    WHILE I NODDED, NEARLY NAPPING,
SUDDENLY THERE CAME A TAPPING,
    AS OF SOMEONE GENTLY RAPPING,
RAPPING AT MY CHAMBER DOOR.
    "'TIS SOME VISITOR," I MUTTERED,
"TAPPING AT MY CHAMBER DOOR—
    ONLY THIS AND NOTHING MORE."

SO BEGINS EDGAR ALLAN POE'S MOST FAMOUS POEM THAT TELLS THE STORY OF A TROUBLED MAN WHO FINDS THAT THE SOUND HE HEARS IS NOT A VISITOR KNOCKING AT HIS BEDROOM DOOR. INSTEAD, IT IS A LARGE PITCH-BLACK RAVEN TAPPING ITS CLAW AGAINST HIS WINDOW. WHEN HE THROWS OPEN THE WINDOW, THE BIRD FLIES IN AND PERCHES ABOVE THE DOOR. THE RAVEN WILL NOT LEAVE. THE MAN GETS MORE AND MORE FRUSTRATED AND ANGRY. HE FEELS AS IF HE IS GOING CRAZY. WHAT'S MORE, THE BIRD WILL ONLY ANSWER HIS QUESTIONS WITH A SINGLE WORD: "NEVERMORE."

THE NARRATOR IS UPSET OVER THE DEATH OF HIS GIRLFRIEND, "A SAINTED MAIDEN WHOM THE ANGELS NAME LENORE." HE WANTS THE RAVEN TO TELL HIM WHEN HE WILL HOLD LENORE AGAIN.

"QUOTH THE RAVEN, 'NEVERMORE.'"

again. Edgar wrote the poem in one room of his New York home, knowing that Virginia was dying in another.

In January of 1847, nearly five years after first coming down with tuberculosis, Virginia died. She was just twenty-four years old. Edgar would hold her nevermore.

Chapter 7
One Final Mystery

After Virginia's death, Edgar was sick and depressed. But he continued to write, particularly poems about beautiful women who die young.

Edgar's final poem was "Annabel Lee." He wrote it in the spring of 1849, but it wasn't published until two days after his death, in October in the *New York Tribune*.

*I was a child and she was a child
in this kingdom by the sea*

*But we loved with a love that was more
than love - I and my Annabel Lee*

Many experts believe Annabel Lee represents Virginia, but others say she represents all the women Edgar knew and loved who died during his lifetime.

"Women have been angels of mercy to me," he said. All of the closest relationships in his life were with women. He made friends with men he worked with, but those friendships—like his jobs—never seemed to last. He eerily predicted in 1848: ". . . unless some true and tender and pure womanly love save me, I shall hardly last a year longer, alone!" He could not stand the thought of being alone and was busy searching for love again.

SARAH HELEN WHITMAN

Edgar was engaged for a short time to the poet Sarah Helen Whitman. However, the marriage was called off when Sarah heard reports that Edgar was drinking too much

and dating other women. Edgar then reunited
with his teenage girlfriend, Elmira Royster,
who was by then a widow with two children.

Her children disapproved of Edgar. And although
Elmira would lose the money she inherited upon
her husband's death if she remarried, she agreed
to marry Edgar. But she had one condition:

Edgar had to promise to stop drinking. To prove he was serious, Edgar joined a temperance society, a club whose members vow never to drink liquor.

In September of 1849, Edgar had been visiting Elmira in Virginia. As he was getting ready to return to New York, he came down with a fever. Edgar went to see a doctor in Richmond before boarding a steamboat there.

But he never made it back to New York. Several days later, on October 3, Edgar was found outside a tavern in Baltimore. He was nearly unconscious, talking nonsense, and was wearing someone else's clothes. No one knows how he got there or where he had been. Edgar was taken to a nearby hospital,

but he never recovered. He died on October 7.

How Edgar arrived at the Baltimore tavern and what happened to him in the days before remain a mystery. Edgar was sick with a fever even before he left for New York. Still, some wild possibilities have been given for his behavior. One is that

Elmira's brothers didn't want her to marry Edgar, so they got him drunk to make it look like he broke his promise.

Another is that he may have already had heart disease or some other illness. Or that he had contracted rabies from an animal bite. Or perhaps Edgar died of alcohol poisoning.

Following Edgar's death, American writer and editor Rufus Griswold wrote a not-so-nice obituary in the *New York Tribune*. He had

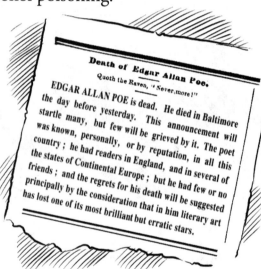

Death of Edgar Allan Poe.

Quoth the Raven, "Nevermore!"

EDGAR ALLAN POE is dead. He died in Baltimore the day before yesterday. This announcement will startle many, but few will be grieved by it. The poet was known, personally, or by reputation, in all this country; he had readers in England, and in several of the states of Continental Europe; but he had few or no friends; and the regrets for his death will be suggested principally by the consideration that in him literary art has lost one of its most brilliant but erratic stars.

never forgotten about a negative review Edgar gave one of his books several years earlier. "Edgar Allan Poe is dead," the obituary began. "He died in Baltimore the day before yesterday.

This announcement will startle many, but few will be grieved by it."

Among other things, Griswold insisted that Edgar had few or no friends, and that he was an angry person who was jealous of other people's success. In a collection of Edgar's works and in other publications, Griswold made up stories that damaged Edgar's reputation even further. He said Edgar roamed the streets talking to himself.

Readers of Edgar's stories knew that he often wrote shocking descriptions of death or violence, and that he sometimes wrote from the point of view of a crazy person. Some of the characters in his stories were drug addicts. So when Griswold wrote such things, people believed them.

Edgar and Griswold had first met in 1841 and were sometimes friends and sometimes rivals. And for twenty-five years after Edgar's death, his reputation was influenced by what Griswold had written and said about him.

It was only after Englishman John Henry Ingram published a fairer and more accurate biography of Edgar in 1875 that people began to accept Edgar for who he was. He was neither crazy nor a drug addict. He was a complex man who struggled to overcome a series of sad events to become a major American writer. He influenced so many writers after him that his work is still studied in high schools, colleges, and universities more than 165 years after his death.

Edgar's status as the father of American mysteries is confirmed by the annual Edgar Allan Poe Awards. "The Edgars," as they are called, are presented by the Mystery Writers of America each year. They honor the best mystery writing in categories such as fiction, nonfiction, short story, young adult, television, and others.

Edgar Allan Poe was a master at writing chilling mysteries. He is the creator of the modern-day detective story and was one of the earliest science-fiction writers. But he also wrote lovely poems and even some humorous stories, too.

In the years since his death, Edgar's popularity has grown beyond his writing. His picture is on action figures, dolls, lunch boxes, bandages, a US postage stamp, and more. He has become an icon—a small thing that represents a bigger idea—of all things spooky and gloomy.

Edgar's poetry, stories, and the mystery surrounding his death all contribute to his legacy as one of the most original American writers of all time. He remains one of the most widely read authors of the nineteenth century. And his work continues to amaze and terrify readers of all ages.

THE BALTIMORE RAVENS

ALTHOUGH EDGAR ALLAN POE WAS BORN IN BOSTON, HE LIVED, WORKED, AND DIED IN BALTIMORE. THE NATIONAL FOOTBALL LEAGUE'S BALTIMORE RAVENS—SUPER BOWL CHAMPS IN THE 2000 AND 2012 SEASONS—TOOK THEIR NAME FROM EDGAR'S POEM "THE RAVEN."

THE TEAM CAME INTO BEING IN 1996. ITS NICKNAME WAS CHOSEN BY FANS OVER TWO OTHER FINALISTS, THE AMERICANS AND THE MARAUDERS, IN A POLL IN THE *BALTIMORE SUN* NEWSPAPER. THE BALTIMORE RAVENS' MASCOT IS A LARGE BLACK BIRD—A RAVEN NAMED POE.

TIMELINE OF
EDGAR ALLAN POE'S LIFE

1809 — Born Edgar Poe on January 19 in Boston, Massachusetts

1811 — Edgar's mother, Eliza Poe, dies at twenty-four
Two-year-old Edgar is taken in by the Allan family of Richmond, Virginia

1815 — Moves to England with his foster parents

1820 — The Allans return to Richmond from England

1826 — Attends the University of Virginia in Charlottesville

1827 — Joins the US Army
Publishes his first book, *Tamerlane and Other Poems*

1829 — Fanny Allan, Edgar's foster mother, dies at forty-four

1830 — Attends West Point but is expelled one year later

1831 — Moves to Baltimore to live with his aunt Maria Clemm, his cousin Virginia Clemm, and his brother, William Henry Poe

1834 — John Allan, Edgar's foster father, dies at fifty-four and leaves Edgar out of his will

1836 — Marries Virginia Clemm on May 16

1838 — The Poes move to Philadelphia

1839 — Begins working as an editor for *Burton's Gentleman's Magazine*

1841 — Writes "The Murders in the Rue Morgue," a short story that creates a new literary category: the detective story

1845 — Publishes his most famous and enduring poem, "The Raven"

1847 — On January 30, Virginia Clemm Poe dies from tuberculosis

1849 — On October 7, Edgar dies at age forty

TIMELINE OF THE WORLD

Founding Father Thomas Jefferson becomes the third president of the United States	1801
The United States doubles in size with the Louisiana Purchase from the French	1803
The first commercial steamboat sails in the United States	1807
Britain and the United States wage the War of 1812	1812
Former French emperor Napoleon returns from exile but is defeated at the Battle of Waterloo	1815
Mexico becomes a republic	1824
Eighteen-year-old Victoria becomes queen of the United Kingdom	1837
Samuel Morse sends the first telegraph message from Washington, DC, to Baltimore	1844
The California Gold Rush begins	1848
The first transatlantic telegraph cable enables nearly instant communication between North America and Europe	1858
Abraham Lincoln is elected the sixteenth president of the United States	1860
The American Civil War begins	1861
President Lincoln issues the Emancipation Proclamation	1863
The American Civil War ends President Lincoln is assassinated	1865

BIBLIOGRAPHY

Ackroyd, Peter. **Poe: A Life Cut Short**. New York: Doubleday, 2008.

Bloomfield, Shelley Costa. **The Everything Guide to Edgar Allan Poe**. Avon, MA: Adams Media, 2007.

* Burlingame, Jeff. **Edgar Allan Poe: Deep Into That Darkness Peering**. Berkeley Heights, NJ: Enslow Publishers, 2008.

* Lange, Karen E. **Nevermore: A Photobiography of Edgar Allan Poe**. Washington, DC: National Geographic, 2009.

* Meltzer, Milton. **Edgar Allan Poe: A Biography**. Brookfield, CT: Twenty-First Century Books, 2003.

* Books for young readers

* Peltak, Jennifer. **Edgar Allan Poe (Who Wrote That?)**. Philadelphia: Chelsea House Publishers, 2004.

Silverman, Kenneth. **Edgar A. Poe: Mournful and Never-Ending Remembrance**. New York: HarperCollins Publishers, 1991.

Sova, Dawn B. **Critical Companion to Edgar Allan Poe: A Literary Reference to His Life and Work**. New York: Facts on File, 2007.

* Streissguth, Tom. **Edgar Allan Poe (A&E)**. Minneapolis: Lerner Publications Company, 2001.

YOUR HEADQUARTERS FOR HISTORY

Activities, Mad Libs, and sidesplitting jokes!
Discover the Who HQ books beyond the biographies

Who? What? Where?

Learn more at whohq.com!